WHAT ARE WORDS OF KNOWLEDGE

BRIAN FENIMORE

Plumbline Ministries
Belton, Mo

Published by Plumbline Publishing
From Plumbline Ministries
Belton, Mo. U.S.A.
www.plumbline.me
Printed in the U.S.A.

All Scripture quotations, unless otherwise indicated, are taken from the New American Standard Bible, by the Lockman Foundation ®. Used by permission.

Copyright ® 2012 Brian Fenimore
All rights reserved. No part of this publication may be reproduced. Stored in a retrieval system or transmitted in any form by any means, electronic, mechanical, photocopy, recording or otherwise, without the prior permission of the publisher, except as provided by USA copyright law.

Content

Table of Contents

Chapter One..3

Trinitian View of Gifts

Chapter Two...29

What Are Words of Knowledge

Content

CHAPTER ONE

TRINITARIAN VIEW OF SPIRITUAL GIFTS

When it comes to gifting, there are three distinct families or categories of gifts that are included in the Bible.

THE MOTIVATIONAL GIFTS OF ROMANS 12

In Romans 12 the Lord inspired Paul to write about what we call the motivational gifts. *"Since we have gifts that differ according to the grace given to us, each of us is to exercise them accordingly: if prophecy, according to the proportion of his faith; if service, in his serving; or he who teaches, in his teaching; or he who exhorts, in his exhortation; he who gives, with liberality; he who leads, with diligence; he who shows mercy, with cheerfulness"* **Romans 12:6-8**. They are how God has made us in our mother's womb. They constitute strong motivation to what we do and our purpose in life.

Whether you know the Lord or not, everybody has a basic bent and natural inclination in their life. We all know people that don't know the Lord yet they are highly motivated for righteous causes. There are people who have a certain clarity about right and wrong, and they tend to see things in black and white in that way. There are also people that have a bent for hospitality.

This is what the Apostle Paul is talking about in Romans 12, and these are the motivational gifts. Whether people ever find the Lord or not, one or more of these tendencies are in everyone. They are evidence of how God has knit us in our mother's womb.

THE SPIRITUAL GIFTS OF 1 CORINTHIANS 12

Then we come into the spiritual gifts listed in **1 Corinthians 12:8-11**: *"For to one is given the word of wisdom through the Spirit, and to another the word of knowledge according to the same Spirit; to another faith by the same Spirit, and to another gifts of healing by the one Spirit, and to another the effecting of miracles, and to another prophecy, and to another the distinguishing of spirits, to another various kinds of tongues, and to another the interpretation of tongues. One and the same Spirit works all these things, distributing to each one individually* *just as He wills."* These are what I call the manifestation gifts of the Holy Spirit. Most people know these as the spiritual gifts, but there are more spiritual gifts listed in the Bible than these, so I don't tend to refer to them that way. These involve God showing forth His glory, and as He does this He gives gifts.

THE LEADERSHIP GIFTS OF EPHESIANS 4

Then we have the gifts that deal with our basic callings and are found in **Ephesians 4:11:** *"And He gave some as apostles, and some as prophets, and some as evangelists, and some as pastors and teachers."* When Jesus ascended to the Throne of God on high, He gave certain gifts to believers. Chiefly, He gave Himself as the greatest gift in a whole new way through the Holy Spirit. He expresses His authority, His kingship and His rule through the gifts of Ephesians 4, and those are office callings referred to as the leadership gifts. Someone might have an office calling gift, but it still takes a lifetime to develop it. If someone has one or more of these gifts, they stand in that office with the very authority of the Lord Jesus Christ to move in that gift, which can done with maturity or immaturity.

Prophecy

There are so many misconceptions of what the prophetic is. Either we make it so hard that no one does it or we blur the term so that everything is prophecy. And there is a distinction of prophecy and that's what I want to explore. So, again, it says here in the introduction, as we come to the gift of prophecy, we see how it shifts from how God is dealing with men. Through prophecy, God is coming to communicate with his people. Prophecy, just like every gift of the spirit, can be ministered by every believer in the local church. Because of the fact that God cares for us, we're called to be his people and that he's given us his spirit, he can speak through all of us a message to strengthen another person.

Now, in the context of where we're at right now, we've enjoyed a certain level of the prophetic and so everyone views the people that have been set apart in that ministry and say, Well, that is the standard; I can't do that. And they've left the simple gift of prophecy. Now, the simple gift of prophecy is actually what we're going to look at, so let's just move on here.

The category of the gift of prophecy. Now, the Greek word is "prophetaya" Now, "prophetaya" is from "pro" and this means "forth." And "phemi" "to speak" When people start coming to prophecy, I don't what any of your background is, but when I first came to prophecy, I thought this is what it meant: it meant that we get in a Bible study and we pull out the Book of Daniel and the Book of Revelation and we get a big bag of chips and a bunch of soda and for the next six hours we're trying to figure out when Gog and Magog are going to come down into israel. And we're always trying to figure out future events all the time, right? That's what I thought prophecy was.

I started studying the gift, there are several aspects of how prophecy is expressed and it's in this whole thing about the word in the Greek.

First, theres forth-telling. There are three aspects of prophecy. Now, forth-telling means this: the presence of the Holy Spirit is upon you to speak. it's not predictive, it's the anointing behind you that, as you speak, God brings the prophetic anointing on it and, if you look at prophecy as it goes through the Old Testament and even into the New Testament, it has several different aspects. it's actually the immediate
voice of God now. And it carries the weight of God's authority and it carries the weight of his demonstration through his voice. But it isn't futuristic. And see, when we started trying to learn how to prophesy . . . to tell each other . . . what usually happened is we would get in a small group and the first thing we would try to do is tell each other what everyone's going to do for the next 20 years of their life.

Now, that is a form of prophecy, but for the beginning level of prophecy you don't want to go there.

Until people get comfortable with the voice of God in their life, they need to know that God loves them. And so, the first levels of prophecy is actually learning to speak God's love to the person and it's under an anointing that you do it.

Now, as we've looked at the story of Nathaniel, when he moved out of word of knowledge and he went right into prophecy, prophecy has the ability, because God has a desire for your life, that when a prophetic word comes, God causes that word to go inside of you just like the power of the resurrection, grab your inner man and cause your will to be transformed in what is spoken to you. Now, we have to look at God's perspective on prophecy, okay?

Not in the predictive element, just in the immediate, "Here, I love you, I want to change your life." Since God is above creation and he's above time and since we were created in time and in creation, we only see things as they go along in the future. What God does is when he comes in prophecy, he sees it all as though it's happening all right now. Because he isn't weighed down by time. And so, when God's telling you something like, what is going on with you or this is how he see you, that's reality. Because you might not be experiencing that now, but the prophetic word is awaking and breaking things off of you so that that will start happening in your life.

So, it has the ability to transform you, that's why it's so powerful. That's why the enemy comes against it so much, is because it's the tool that God uses, his very voice, to communicate his heart.

Alright, that is not a big deal in the aspect that if you see it from the perspective that God is a father. As I have little children and I look at my children, I have desires in my heart for that child to live a certain way and I speak that way to that child. I pronounce blessings over them, I speak to them and I try to encourage values that are godly. Well, God's the father over our lives. So, what God does is he takes his children and he uses you in the aspect that he shows you something that's in his heart which he wants to happen in their life, he shows it to you, you prophesy it to the person so that they will know what direction they're supposed to go so that the blessing of what God wants to come in the future will avalanche into their life.

Now, that's just two elements of prophecy. Now, here's another -- this is just a simple gift -- here's another element: The highest form of prophecy that the Lord Jesus Christ has given us today is not talking about judgment. In the Old Testament all they had was God coming upon them, They didn't have the Spirit living inside of them. That was actually their biggest hang-up, is that they didn't have the

Spirit of God living inside of them. They were not a new creation, so they were always in sin. Naturally, if you don't have God inside of you, you're going to live in sin, right? When Jesus Christ came he switched prophecy.

Now, the Spirit lives in all of you and your greatest, your highest demonstration, of prophesying to people is to reveal my Father. See, that's what Jesus did. Jesus, if you look at how he prophesied in the New Testament, he always told them what God thought about them, not just what their future was and stuff like that, that's most of his prophetic ministry and then every once in a while he'd say, Yeah, see the temple is going to fall down some day.

It isn't that Jesus doesn't talking about the future, but the thing that you really need to know is that God loves you and has a plan for your life. He's your Father and he's never going to leave you or forsake you ever. And that's the perspective of prophecy, even the simple gift of prophecy that we have to take a bite out of, because we all want to know the future, but without relationship, why do you care? You see, Jesus Christ is saying, This life which is my Father is what you need and so I'm going to prophesy out of that so it will change you to get ready to face the future.

I used to think here's the cool thing about prophecy if I could get in a room and have whole bunch of people lay hands on me and tell me what's going to happen in the next five years, it would answer all the questions I have in my life. After I got around that for awhile, I started realizing that even though they tell you, I'd still walk out of the room, going, Well, I still don't know what to do. And I still don't have the grace to live this thing out. I've got to have something more substantial. And realized that prophecy is to cause you to know that God cares for your future, but it's always to cause you to go back to him.

Jesus wants you to forth-tell his word and fore-tell his word in the greatest dimension to reveal his Father. And that's where prophecy is today.if you see the prophetic ministry like a lot of people do, what prophecy is like in the Old Testament, you'll never be able to embrace prophecy. Because you'll see Elijah run up on the hills and say, "Are you going to serve God or Baal? Right?" And this was what Israel . . . and the nation . . . it was a divine act that God was going to do, but God today is saying, Israel is not the most important thing. I am.

And he's confronting people individually and he's not taking on just Israel anymore, he's taking on the whole world. And where we want to see lightening come to straighten out the people, that's actually what Jesus judged in his disciplines all the time, that attitude. You remember when they were walking along as disciples and they said, "Lord, they didn't obey us, let's call fire down from heaven and destroy the city." That's most of what I would consider prophecy in the church today. I mean, it's embarrassing to say that, but we just don't have a heart of love and Jesus said, "You don't know what you're saying, what kind of spirit you're speaking out of."

Now see, Jesus knew his Father and he realized, "My greatest desire is to reveal the love of God to this person and I'm going to use all of the gifts of the spirit to do that." What we do is we get tired of the world and we think prophecy is the tool I can use to judge the heck out of mankind. Now, I know I'm going hard and fast, so let's look at the Bible. John 1:50. Now, we've used this story as the understanding of revelation, but let me say something to you. I'm using this story because it has all the elements of the gifts. And here it has the gift of prophecy. in verse 50, the reason I use this, is this is where Jesus is turning, in this scripture, he's not giving information any more, he's telling them, here's what you're going to be doing for the Lord. it says,

"Jesus answered and said, Because I said I saw you under the fig tree do you believe? You shall see greater things than these. And then he said to him, "Truly, I say to you, you shall see the heavens open . . . ."

He's telling Nathanal his future right here. My Father so loves you that the heavens are going to be opened and the angels of God are going to ascend and descend on the Son of Man. He tells him all this revelation knowledge so that the heart will open so that the love of God and the calling and the destiny that God wants to speak into you will come, meet you and you'll embrace it. it's an awesome thing God does in prophecy.

Here's where I finally started seeing the distinction of the gift of prophecy. For a long time I blurred word of knowledge, word of wisdom, discerning of spirits and prophecy. I just kind of blurred them like this and I just kind of went for the package all the time, right? And I know it's hard to bring a distinction, so I'm going to show you, alright?

This minister and I went to a conference called the Ohio Prophetic Conference. We were doing a session on prophecy. All I was doing, actually, was just sitting there listening to him tell his stories and then he'd bring me up to pray for people.

It was time to do ministry and I heard the Lord clearly just indicate to me in a simple phrase in my brain, "Don't tell them where they live." And I thought, "What" I thought the prophetic ministry was so that you would know that I know your shoe size and what your favorite ice cream is and what your uncle Fred's name is. And I started thinking that the greater gift of prophecy was to tell you everything about all you've ever done, all you ever thought about. And the Lord said, "That's actually the gift of the word of knowledge. You prophesy to them and I thought, "Well, what does that mean?"

And all of a sudden I hear this scripture coming into my mind. "See how much love the Father has lavished on us that we should be called the children of God and such we are." And so, he said, I want you to stand here for the next five minutes and that's what I did -- for the next five minutes we went tandem back and forth, just talking about how much God loved them.

Now, I've been in some meetings that I thought were interesting, but I've never seen anything like this. When we started not telling them, I didn't go, You. You have a sister, you've been praying this . . . I blew all that off and I said, "Here's what the Lord's showing me, that he loves you and that he'll take care of you and that his heart is towards you." And all we did was just started doing that. I used terms like this: Have you ever gone out side and laid in the summer and tried to get a sun tan and you fall asleep and your face is saturated and burned? That's what I was experiencing that day, under God's presence.

I literally broke out in a sweat and I felt like I was getting a glory sunburn. I mean, my body was just racked with heat and I'm just like, "Ahhhh." As we're doing this, I've seen word of knowledge break people and all that other stuff -- but when the purest form of prophecy comes,

God's love and affirmation and his tenderness towards people, it almost becomes scary to be in the room. Because we want to hope that God cares for us, but when God is actually telling us that he does, it doesn't just have the weight behind it of words, it has the weight of revelation, it has the weight of glory coming near you and it starts changing you the minute that it comes near you.

So, we're just, I'm trying to stay focused and hear this, and periodically I'm tracking my eyes to see what's going on in the crowd. This guy, I still have to touch myself, because I can't believe it happened, but this guy back in the back row was sitting in his chair and all I'm doing is saying, "See how much love the Father lavished on us?" And I'm just saying that scripture.

Somehow the Holy Spirit picks him up out of his chair, flips over in back of him and knocks the whole row in back of him out, just "wham." And I'm just watching that going, "Wow, that's different." And I remember looking at the other minister and I was trying to say with my eyes, "Did you just see that?" And it kind of threw me for a minute and so the other minister just started talking about that God will never leave you or forsake them and we're just prophesying, saying simple words under the anointing. This guy up in the row up here stands up and at the top of his lungs starts screaming, "Ahhhhh." Like that and just "wham" falls on the ground like a sack of potatoes.

And I'm just watching him, going "Wow!" And I'm feeling the intensity of the Holy Spirit just pounding on the room.

I saw the reason why God gave gifts of revelation was to get you awakened to the fact that he's there, but prophecy has more weight behind it, that's why Paul's telling us to head towards that gift. Because it's the creative force of God's voice and he uses you as an instrument and it changes and transforms and delivers people immediately. The prophetic anointing is just like it was in the time of israel. That's why God called his judges prophets. Because when they spoke it was under the anointing of prophecy and it changed people's lives. It set the course of a nation. Now, God has released that awesome, powerful giftedness through all of us. isn't that amazing? And we're waiting for one guy to go do it . . . "Oh, if we just could go hear that one person give a prophetic word . . ." We've got to get past that.

Now, I'm sitting here reading the Book of Galatians, sitting there just overwhelmed by the fact that God is saying that we are not children any more. We are sons. And that this gospel has been given to us . . . and then this word he used for "son" was not talking about a little infant.

He's talking about a mature person. And so, what he's saying is that everything that you need to function just like the Old Testament prophets and prophesy to each other the Father's given you and you can do it.

Now, I know that we have prophets and we have prophetic ministry, but God calls us all to do this.

So, let's move on and look at some other examples. Let's go to John 4:17 -24 and I'm pretty sure this is the woman at the well and we've already looked at this, but . . . Okay, now in verse 17, obviously we're covering the same ground where it's talking about that she has no husband. Then he gives her a word of knowledge and that blows here away so that she thinks he's a prophet just from saying that.

But, as the scripture progresses, she goes to her greatest question which is, "You say we're supposed to worship, you know, here in Kansas City, other ones say we're supposed to worship in California, where are we supposed to worship?" And what Jesus says to her is, I'm going to prophesy to you right now, here's the highest form of what you need to know. My Father is a Spirit and you will worship him in spirit and truth.i That's a prophetic word to her. Because he's setting the course of her life by telling her that. He's speaking something into her, he's speaking life. And when he does that, it pierces her and makes her go into town and say, "Come and see a man who told me everything I ever did.' Just by that simple revelation, "My Father is who you're going to worship." That was a powerful prophetic word to her.

That's why Christ carried it, it had his blessing on it, because he was saying, "You know what, you don't need to know what you're going to do next week. That's not as important as that I'm immediate to you and I so love you that I'm going to be the life force that you draw from.

"Now, when I'm tired, I see a progression going when I prophesy to people. When I'm tired and I don't feel the life of God inside of me to prophesy, I get stuck in an avenue of word of knowledge. And for some people that's just enough. They're so overwhelmed that God would even give that information, but when you're really hitting the heart of God's love, you can prophesy and it's an incredibly deep well that you could just rest in.

Here's another example: went to Guatemala. I got sick. I did everything I could do to keep from getting sick and I still got sick. We're starting to minister to a lady. Now, I had to speak through an interpreter, so it makes it a little harder, but I pointed out a lady in the crowd and I said, "Would you stand, please?" And she stood, and I said, " I saw this little girl standing right next to her, Your oldest daughter has black hair, right?" And she says, "Yeah." Now, see that . . . how could she not . . . I mean, they're from Guatemala, okay? But there are some people that don't have black hair in Guatemala, okay, so I figured there was a little revelation there and I said, "Your daughter drives you up the wall, doesn't she?" And she looked at the interpreter and the interpreter looked at me and they said, "What does 'drive up the wall' mean?" And I thought, "Oh, there's one of those American, silly phrases," and I thought, "Okay, she didn't get that did she?" And she goes, that lady said, "No." And I said, "Tell her that the daughter gets on her nerves." And so, she said, "Your daughter . . .I and you know. And the lady said, "Yes." And then she was all happy. I mean, that wouldn't really like wake me up.

But she starts crying and I notice, "Oh, my gosh, look at that. God's going to love on her.' Now, right there I had to make a decision, am I going to try to blow her away with more information, because God gave me more information, or am I going to stop and dip into the heart of God's love for this lady? So, I thought, you know I'm going to just dip into his love for a moment.
When I took the plunge into God's love, there was a river that anywhere I wanted to go with this lady in this child relationship, he was going to give information and touch that lady. I said, "Your child has the same gifting that you have. She's an intercessor. That's why she gets on your nerves. She's just like you." And this lady says, "Yes! Yes! Yes!" And I said, and God has his hand on her and he has a call on her life and I mean, the information was just so

fresh. it was just like a fruit falling from the tree and you could just eat it. Now, why did God give me that?

Because I stayed in the heart of love. I wasn't trying to blow everyone away with information any more, I was touching the deepest need that was in her life and that was that God would bring someone all the way from the United Sates to tell you that he loves you and he's going to take care of your child. Now, the minute I backed off on that and I thought, "Wow, this is really cool. I think I'll tell her some other stuff." I missed his heart of love for her. Then it started becoming dry word of knowledge again. You see the aspect I'm trying to communicate here? See, prophecy, the deepest form of it, is revealing the love of God to people.

They have got to know he cares for them. That's why we never evaluate prophecy by the amount of information. It's the amount of God's love that's being transferred into that person's heart. The first few times I started doing this, all I could get was, "God loves you." And we'd all laugh, "Isn't he giving you anything else?" "Can't you grow in the prophetic ministry? I mean, doesn't God have anything else he wants to tell you, like God's going to grab you and you're going to be translated and you don't even have to use airplanes, he's going to take you from here to there and angels are going to be with you every day of the week, and God's going to visit you for 20 weeks, and all he's going to tell you, is the end of the world, day after day. I mean, can't you get that stuff?" That's important, but it's not as important . . . You know, I could tell you a bunch of things under the anointing of the Holy Spirit, but if you don't know God loves you, you won't accept them.

Do you realize that? If I sit here and say, "God wants to do this and this and this with you." And you sit back and you think, "Well, I thought God hated me." It won't mean anything to you. So, the depth of prophecy is not the information. The depth of prophecy is that they get the impartation of God's Father heart of love that transforms them.

Okay, let's go to John 12. Now, this whole story revolves around the fact that the Greeks are now getting the idea that Jesus is the Messiah and they want to start having meetings with him. And so, he gives this parable about grain falling to the ground. If it doesn't fall to the ground, it can't produce any other kind of crop, alright? And he's kind of telling it in a parabolic form that he needs to die so this thing that he has living inside of him, this dynamic of life, would go to all of mankind.

Then, he says,

"Now, as my sole has become troubled, what shall I say? Father, save me from this hour? But for this purpose

I came to this hour. Father, glorify thy name. Then, therefore, a voice out of heaven said, I have both glorified it and I will glorify it again. And the multitude therefore stood by and heard it and were saying that it thundered. Others saying an angel had spoke to him. And Jesus answered, This voice has not come for my sake but for your sake. Now, judgment is upon this world. Now, the ruler of this world has been cast out and I, if I am lifted up from the earth, I will draw all men to myself."

Here's what I'm trying to communicate with prophecy. Jesus Christ is judging only one thing now the activity of the enemy. The bondage that's in mankind. And he's saying that the prophetic ministry has to go from you telling people God's going to nail them to the point where you accurately say, God's going to nail the enemy in your life and you need to have the prophetic ministry, the prophecy coming out of your mouth lifting up the Lord Jesus Christ.

You know, in Daniel, he starts having visions. Now, visions are great. I want to have as many as I can before I die, alright. But that isn't the end of all things. As all these visions . . . and then he sees the Son of Man sitting on the throne. See, all that we do has to lift up the Son of God and when you get people where their focus and attention comes off of giftedness or goofiness or silliness back on to him, the release and the impartation of life is going to come into that person and is going to change them.

Now, I've spent all week talking with one person after another and reading several books on this fact: in ministry, even what we're learning to do here with the gifts of the spirit, do we want to just tell people cute information that entertains? See, I'm looking . . . I don't know about you guys, but I'm not looking for information anymore. I'm just tired of information. Now, see, information comes by seeing him, tasting him, eating him, partaking of him then you're changed. If you can see him, you'll be changed from glory to glory. If glory touches you, and that's what prophecy's supposed to do. I'm not trying to make it mystical, but I'm going to paint a picture for you now. If I start prophesying to you and the heavens open up to you and you sense, "God is with me right now," it will cause you to receive everything that's being said to you.

You'll receive it at a deeper level, past your presuppositions. It will go into your spirit like a seed. And the very thing that you resist against God, God will plant in you with a prophetic word. And then one morning you're now having dreams and you wake up and you say, "I remember this person said I was going to have dreams." Now, that's not the end of all things, but that's awakened inside of you and it causes you to realize that God is so in control that the Lord Jesus Christ can cause things to happen in my life through this prophetic word to make my life a beautiful thing.

I can learn to partake of that thing, just by prophesying to each other. Now, I know I'm getting really kind of loud on this stuff, but I need to say something. A lot people say, " I don't hear God."I struggle hearing God." God releasing prophecy to you is not up to you to try to hear him.

It's based on grace. And I realize that I keep presenting to you guys, you've got to be able to get this, you've got to be able to get this, and I feel that weight coming on you as I'm saying that.

Now, I used to sit around and look at my teachers when they'd say that to me and I'd think, "Yeah, but how? How? How? First, it's by asking for grace to be released that you can hear. See, you don't grow in prophecy because you learn the skill of it. That's part of it.

You learn it by grace being released in you. And that's what we're going to pray. I'm actually going to pray for this to be released in all of you today. And listen. It's something . . . you can't . . . you can learn all the mechanics you want, but what you're wanting to do is you're wanting to get before your Father and say, "Reveal your love to me. Let me have a revelation of this stuff. Let me have a revelation of your voice. Let me grow in the ability to hear you." See, because, I'm trying for years posturing myself and meditating and studying scriptures and it still didn't make his voice more accessible to me. Then when I started saying, "Reveal your love to me." Well, there his voice was all the time. Acts 13. Now, there are several different ways that the gifts of the Spirit work and we're going to talk about this and this is the good lead in to begin with this.

Now, in Acts 13, obviously the church is starting to flourish. And it says,

"Now, there were in Antioch in the church there were prophets and teachers, Barnabus and Simeon, who was called Niger, and Lucius the Cyrene. They had been brought up from Herod, the tetrarch, and Saul. While they were ministering to the Lord and fasting the Holy Spirit said, set apart for me Barnabas and Saul for the work I have called them. Then when they had fasted and prayed, they laid their hands on them and sent them on their way."

Now, the first way that I see prophecy starting to happen in our lives is this -- I already started talking about it -- that you come before God and you realize, unless you start worshipping through me there won't be access for me to know you. And so, you ask the Holy Spirit, "Worship through me." And as you start getting into a life of worship, it is literally kissing your Father. Now, I don't know about you, but I have little kids. When my girls sit on my lap and give me a kiss, I'm melted butter. Anything they want. "Dad, can I run over you with the car?" "Yes." "Just give me another kiss." And when you . . . see, God is so for you, that when you worship him, you're literally expressing love to him. And you're kissing him. Now, he's not the big Santa Claus in heaven, but he's pretty close to that. He really thinks you're great. And when you come back and you say, "You know, I just love you." He just sits there and goes, "God, I'm broken over you. I want to come back and I want to kiss on you." Then he comes back with his voice. That's one of the ways he kisses you back.

So, they worshiped and then the Holy Spirit said, "Set apart these guys." Now, they laid hands on them. Here's the first way that prophecy comes - laying on of hands. Now, I'm going to talk to you about several different ways that prophecy comes. The first one about laying on of hands is this: Now, I'm going to speak a paradox to you, because I'm going to say something and then I'm going to contradict it, okay? Sometimes when you feel nothing . . . now, let's all admit something . . . a lot of how we think we're supposed to move in the gifts of the Spirit is feeling. I hang out with prophetic people all the time and I listen to the things they say to me and they'll say this, "I don't feel anything." Alright. Do you hear that? So they won't minister. Now, that's wrong in the aspect of this: Jesus Christ said, "Go, make disciples of all nations." So, that "Go" word is resting on you all the time and you're supposed to go whether you feel like it or not, okay?

Now, when people are hurting and you still don't feel like ministering to them, that's supposed to cause you to look at that person and have your heart broken by the presence of God, because there should be something of God's life in you, whether you feel like it or not, that when a person's hurting you want to reach and you want to give to them. And so, most of the time when I don't feel like prophesying . . . and we've done this in class, when I've said, "I don't feel anything." You've heard me say that.

We often think we're supposed to move in hthe gifts of the Spirit by feeling, but Jesus said" Go make disciples of all nations." That "go" is a command we're to go out of obedience not feeling. When the Spirit is in you He can give you a desire to reach out and touch people when they're hurting whether you feel like ti or not. When they come to us and we lay hands on them, God can use that as an avenue to release His love through us. If we desire to comfort them and bless them with the Father's heart for them, prophecy will come. If you don't feel you're hearing any thing just begin by telling them "God loves you, He cares about what's going on in your life." When you begin this way, God honors that. Then the anointing of God is released thru you to them and awakens the discerning of spirits in you.

I've tried to analyze it as I've done it over and over and over again and I've noticed that, whether you feel like it or not, when you go and lay hands on a person, God awakens. And you start discerning stuff if you just take a moment. You know, remember, when I said you can't take the information you're given and just reject it like it's nothing? When you lay hands on someone you may begin to feel sorrow or fear. Don't think it's your problems and that disqualifies you to minister to them. Rather, it's the Spirit of God resting on you so yo can discern what they're feeling and hear what God whats to speak to them thru you.

Now, as you lay hands on them, discerning of spirits awakens and you feel the pain that people are carrying, it causes the prophetic to come, because God is a Father of love and he wants to speak to that issue. So, he wants you to feel that. Does anyone like this yet? This is the difficult part. When yo sese the pain someone is carrying it can feel overwhelming because of our own problems and we don'tt want to experience another level of it. If we allow the Spirit to work in our soul, it will break us and when that happens the life of God will flow thru us to meet their needs. That is what God wants. When we are desperate and fully depend

on Him the grace and love of the Father will come and
He'll speaks to us.

WORKING WITH WORDS OF KNOWLEDGE

I once had a little picture of a person sitting in a meeting in this old church. I stopped, rested under the presence of God and started asking specific questions. When God shows you a picture, it means you're been given a invitation to go thru the door of grace and rest under the spirit of revelation to receive whatever the Lord wants to reveal in that situation. Many want to know how to receive more accurate words of knowledge. If you will learn to rest in His presence and dwell on the simple things He show you, He will begin to give you more specific information. What happens is that you have a word of knowledge.

It usually comes very quickly. If you don't pay attention to it, you'll just bypass it and you'll miss the grace of God that God actually has for that thing right there. See, if God shows you a picture, it means that you've been given an invitation to go through the door of grace and rest under the spirit of revelation and receive as much as God wants to give over that one situation. A lot of people say, "How do I get more accurate in words of knowledge or how do I get more accurate in hearing the voice of God?" The very simple things that he shows you, if you just dwell on that and let God keep you in a place where you're under his presence, he will start giving you specific information. Now, when I saw the picture of the guy walking to the church, all I said to the Lord was, "I see that, what do you want to say to me about it?" He said, "I'm taking this guy back to his roots." Now, I knew the person and I knew what his roots were. And see, immediately I found my mind going, "That's too simple. I'm not going to say anything about it.

Because everybody already knows all of this." So we went back to the meeting and I thought, "Well, I'm going to have some fun anyway, because it's in my house and if I make a total idiot out of myself, I can go hide in my bedroom." So, I just said to this person, "You know, I feel like the Lord just dropped a picture in me and he said something to you about going back to your roots." Now, it might not have looked like this to everyone else, but it looked like this to me when I was watching me saying it to him and it looked like someone slapped him. He turned his head sides ways. He said, "Man, that's unreal, because the

Lord just told me that." And he said he started doing stuff like that.

Now, once he said that and the information was correct, I found that the spirit of revelation and my own faith started working together and all of a sudden I was caught under a flow of ministering to him just words of knowledge. I saw this, and I then I saw this and then I saw this and it was amazing watching God build that. Just by that simple little picture and once I focused on it and decided to go with it, I got caught under the spirit of revelation.

Now, that's what Jesus is trying to saying here, is that you can come into a place where God will show you the heart of somebody. Now, I know that there's a natural struggle that's going on with you guys here when it comes to giftedness. It's the struggle that all of us walk through. And it's the ability of knowing that God wants you to be here and you're right here. And the struggle it takes to get to that place. I'm still under a constant learning curve in my life on giftedness. I believe that it is something that I have to spend the rest of my life actually being trained continuously, because it's something that you cannot perfect. And so I just take the steps of trying to learn to do this stuff.

Now, first God can move in the natural realm of what we have called finances, family and other ? arenas

and then he can move in the realm of knowing people's hearts or perceiving them. Now see, God wants us to grow in the place where we can perceive the heart of people and not get blind sided by things because we don't have knowledge about it. And so,
he'll show you the hearts of men so that you will not get caught in deception or abuse or any of those arenas. And it comes as discerning of spirits and then the release of knowledge of what you are discerning.

Now, let's go to Mark 9:21-25. Okay, now we're hitting this stuff with healing with words of knowledge, so let's just look at this. Actually, to give you a better background of what's going on, let's go to verse 21. Obviously, you know Jesus has just gotten transfigured. He comes down the mountain and the disciples are trying to cast a demon out of a child. They're not very successful at it and then that's kind of how we pick up the story. The father and the child come towards Jesus. It says here in verse 21,

He asks his father, "How long has this been happening to him?" And he said, "From childhood. And it has often thrown him both into the fire and into the water to destroy him. But if you can do anything, take pity on us and help us. And Jesus said, If you can. All things are possible for him who believes. Immediately, the boy's father cried out and began saying, I do believe. Help my unbelief. And Jesus saw that the crowd was rapidly gathering. He rebuked the unclean spirit and said to it, You deaf and dumb child ?. I command you to come out of him and do not enter him again. And after crying out and throwing himself into terrible convulsions, it came out and the boy became so much like a corpse that most of them said, He is dead. But Jesus took him by the hand and raised him and he got up. And when he had come into the house, his disciples began questioning him privately, Why could we not cast it out? And he said to them, This kind cannot come out by anything but prayer. And then some versions say, "prayer and fasting."

Now, here's the interesting thing that's going on. As you start learning to do ministry. Ministry has models that you can embrace for awhile while you are trying to learn the presence of the Holy Spirit. But models will not always produce results. Models are good to get trained in, but models will not always produce the result you are looking for. And why he's saying, "This kind only comes out by prayer," is he's saying, you have to have intimate relationship to know how to deliver people of certain things. You have to be able to be in a place where God can commune with you and communicate with you. And the disciples had gotten to the place where they knew the model of ministry. And so, instead of getting in touch with the Father and finding out how do we deliver this child, or what are we supposed to say to this child, they knew of model of ministry because Jesus had already sent them out on mission trips.

And so they said, Well, we'll just go back to the model and that's why they couldn't get the demon out. Now, models are good up until the point where they stop helping people. See, if you embrace the model and you don't get in touch with how God speaks or how he releases words, the type of ministry you're going to do is going to flourish for a while and then God will allow the model to fail to show you the model is only a container that carries his presence.

And he wants you really to have relationship with him. Now, this happened when I was trying to learn the five-stage healing model that they were talking about through the Vineyard. After a while the model started working so well that I stopped praying. I would just go into ministry, and say, "Well, the model works so well, that I'll stop talking to God about it."

The problem was that after a while the model stopped helping people, because I stopped relationship and embraced a formula to help people. A formula without God's presence actually does not do any form of ministry. It actually becomes a bondage in your life. And so you have to allow models to give you a place to hear him, learn to move with him, but then you need to go beyond the model back to relationship. And so, that's what Jesus is running into here.

The reason the disciples could not deliver the child of a demon is because they did not get a word of knowledge on it. See, they were going towards a model and they weren't hearing how God wanted them to deal with it. It wasn't because they didn't have faith in the Lord Jesus Christ. They had a faith more in their method than they did in hearing him and doing what he had communicated. Now, I've studied a lot of different models and I've come to the place of realizing, we have to hear God correctly to do effective ministry. It almost doesn't matter what the model is anymore. It's hearing him and what he wants to do in a situation.

In fact, God started destroying my models about the third year I was traveling with another minister. One time I tried to, "Okay, does anyone feel the Lord on you?" And people would just sit there and look at me and I tried to do all the models that I did and no one ever responded. And then I heard the Holy Spirit say, "Just blow real loud into the microphone."

Now, if you guys know me well enough, you know that I try to veer away from that as much as I can. You know, I'm not into shaking and screaming. Well, I am in private, but in public I try to back away from it. And so, I remember this fight I had in my mind with the Lord. And I said, "You know, that's too Pentecostal." Now, I found that God locked me up. That was the word of knowledge and if I wasn't willing to go the direction he wanted to go, he wasn't going to release the results. And so, I just stood up there and everyone thought I was trying to really hear the Lord and all I was doing was fighting with him. "I don't want to do that, God." Finally, I just in a very wimpish way, just went like that real quick. And everyone went, "I wonder what's wrong with the .. system." And nothing happened and I thought, "Oh, I've got to do this whether I want to." And so I took time and I said, "You know, I'm going to do something that's kind of charismatic here, I'm going to blow into the microphone for a minute." So, I just went [loud blowing sound into microphone]. And finally, because that's what the prescription that God gave through a word of knowledge, the person was delivered right there and healed.

Now, for the life of me, I did not want to do that. I'm not into wanting to do that kind of stuff, but that's what God said he was going to use. And remember there's a level of foolishness that comes with this. Because it isn't about me, me looking good. Me having a band, me having a jacket. All that other stuff. And if you look at how the Lord did his ministry, there was a lot of what mankind would consider foolishness which was actually the wisdom of God. You know, boy, one of the ones that really blew me out of the water is when the Lord gets a word that he's supposed to spit on a guy's tongue ?.

You know, we kind of look at it and we just think it's ridiculous, but God told him to spit on the ground and make mud with his fingers and cram it into a guy and he'll see. Right? I mean we look at the ones that are easy for us to embrace, but those, especially when it moves towards the miraculous. I actually travel with another person that moves in the miraculous and God makes him do stuff all the time he doesn't want to do.

Like kick people in the legs when their legs are hurting. And you think, "Well, why would God do that?" "Well, I don't know." But the person doesn't feel it and then they're immediately healed.

In fact, one of the most shocking ones is when this lady actually had an abortion and she was bleeding and she couldn't get control of it, so the Lord told him to slug her in the stomach. And he goes, "You know, I don't really want to do this, but the Lord's told me to punch you in the stomach." She goes, "Go for it." She just put her hands up in the air. And he said, "Well, I decided that if I'm going to do this, I'm just going to drive my fist into her stomach." So he backed off and punched her as hard as he could in the stomach. And he said it was like hitting a bowl of jelly.

His hand just went [jelly sound]. And she says, "Well, when are you going to do it?" And he goes, "Well, I just did it." So she ran off into the bathroom and came back and she was completely healed.

Now, the knowledge that God gives is the way that he's going to do it to bring glory to this name. So, I'm not telling you, now, let's embrace a wild theology of punching and slapping everybody. But, there are going to be times where God is going to stretch your culture and your understanding of what he can do and how he can do it. And he's going to ask you to do things. Now, please here's a key to this. Make sure it's really the voice of the Lord before you do that kind of stuff. And make sure you've walk in some arenas of hearing him in other arenas before you're ready to pull people out of wheelchairs. Okay? Not because God doesn't do that, but you need to make sure it's really him.

It's just the best safeguard that I have for this kind of stuff.Now, let's go to 2 Kings 4:3-7. This is actually the story again of a famine in the land and Elisha telling this widow to do something to actually get money to pay for something. And it says here in verse 3:

"Then he said, Go, and borrow vessels at large for yourself from all your neighbors. Even empty vessels. Do not get a few. You shall go and shut the door behind you and your son and pour out into these vessels and you shall set aside what is full. So she went from him and shut the door behind her and her son. And they were bringing the vessels to her and she poured. And it came about when the vessels were full that she said to her sons, "Bring me another vessel.' And he said to her, "There is not one vessel more.' And the oil stopped."

This woman had a need in her life Elisha go a word of knowledge of how to meet that need thru the Supernatural abundance of God's provision. Thru His strategy, God's kingdom will invade this natural world and reveal how He wants to solve the problem. Most of the time His solution is nothing like what we could do or could imagine. And most of the time the way that God solves problems is not the way that we think he should solve them. In the arena of just money ñ because my wife and I live by faith (and that's kind of what we do with our life) every month we get put in a position when there's always a shortfall. And so, I'm getting to the point where I'm learning this every month now. God wants me to seek him and find out what he's going to do. Right? But it never makes it easy for me, because I'm always stressed. I'm running around the house like a chicken with his head cut off for three or four days until God tackles me and finally I can go before him and go, "Well, what's the strategy here?

How do you want to do this? What is your wisdom on this situation?" And a lot of his wisdom . . . sometimes he'll just say, "Just wait. The provision of the Lord's going to come." Or he'll work out some strategy where something will break and I hate this and where something will break. Someone will come along to help and then they'll see that we're in dire straight and then the provision of God comes that way.   I mean, I hate how he does it some times, but that's the strategy of the Lord for working out situations in our life. Now let's go to Matthew 17:27. Now this is real interesting. They're getting in an argument about money and paying tax. So now they need money. And it says,

"Jesus spoke to him first, saying, 'What do you think, Simon? From whom do the kings of the earth collect customs or pole taxes? From their sons or from strangers?' And upon his saying 'From strangers,' Jesus said to him: 'consequently, the sons are exempt. But lest we give them offense, go to the sea, throw in a hook and take the first fish that comes up and when you open its mouth you will find a starter ? Take that at give it to them for you and me.'"

Now, I don't know about you, but this story just amazes me and that's all a word of knowledge. Just go and catch a bunch of fish. Grab the first one you can. Pop open

What Are Words of Knowledge

his mouth and pull out a coin. And that'll pay taxes for you. I mean, is that a word of knowledge for you or what? And yet, see, if there's an example of it being given in the New Testament, realize: God has given that because he wants you to realize is that that same thing of how God is going to meet things in your life are going to come through words of knowledge.

It's going to be played out not in the way that the kingdom of this world works. Which is: you work real hard and then there's a paying of it. Because God's kingdom is so free, part of the way that he meets most of our crises is to show us that's by grace. So, he makes us do something that seems totally contradictory to the way that we were brought and the way our culture embraces things. And he releases not only words of knowledge on how to do it, but it's also a demonstration of his father's heart. Now let's talk about areas that the gift works. Now, we started this last week, but I need to talk about this. Seeing pictures or visions in the mind's eye. Okay, I'm going to draw on the board now. Here's how words of knowledge come. Depending on what you're doing when you're starting to minister to people, God drops pictures in your mind.

Now, obviously, this is an easy way of getting words of knowledge. Let's say you're laying hands on a person, you close your eyes and all of a sudden this picture comes. I see a picture of usually the gift the the Lord has given them. And it's some of the ways that I've seen it, right? I close my mind and here's this person standing before me and right here I'll see like a little thing that you see when you see comic books, okay? You know, you'll have that thing and then all the captions are in it? And I'll see something like, well, I don't want to get too, but actually a father pointing his finger at a little boy and screaming and yelling at him and I'm feeling the pain of this child, and I'm seeing all of this in a picture, right?

Now, obviously, I'm standing before an adult, so I know that that's not right now. It's when they were a child. So that has to be from their past. If I'll stay focused on this and I'll say, "Okay, I see that and I feel the pain here," God uses that as actually a springboard to show me other visions, okay. So what will happen is, God in these kind of experiences draws your attention even in the experience to what he wants you to focus on, if you'll take time to look at it. And what happens is that in one situation it was the child I was supposed to focus on, not the dad being abusive to the child.

Now what he started telling me was right here, and right next to it, another vision came up. Okay, here's this father yelling at this kid. I go, "Wow, that's interesting. What do you want me to know about that?" He shows me another picture in my mind's eye, where now this kid is growing up and he's got chains ? all over him from this experience. Right? Now, I'm still not hearing words, per se, I'm just seeing pictures, right? Now, this doesn't have anything to do with prophecy. This is just word of knowledge. That's it. I go: "What is that? Okay, I see that. They have chains on them. What are you wanting to tell me?" Now, if you're under the spirit of revelation and he's starting to show you stuff like that, that's where you can be in a place of rest to hear his voice, when a vision or revelation comes. Because you're under a place where you're getting caught up by pictures, but you say, "Well, what is that?" It seems like you're under the flow of revelation. So, all the access of revelation is given. You're not just getting pictures. You're actually under the place where you can hear God's voice too. So, when you are in a place of dialoguing with God, when you see this stuff, you're actually standing . . . what I . . . there are many illustrations you can give. You're at the table of the Lord. You're communing with God. You're in God's manifest presence. You're abiding in the vine.

So, if you're in that place, you are just about to do ministry, the Holy Spirit is looking for how he can touch that person's life and so what he does is he gives you specific pictures so you'll ask him a question: "Okay, that's great. I see the chains. What am I to do with it?" See, when I'm trying to start growing and doing personal ministry or when I started trying to grow in words of knowledge, I hit the wall that you guys all are talking to me about right now, is this: God shows you a real weird picture and you don't know what to do with it.

I think God's ten times more creative than Walt Disney, because I've seen so many weird pictures that I started walking out of ministry experiences going: "I don't know what means." And even if I do know what that means, what am I supposed to do with it? And see, that's where you stay in a place of being a disciple. Now, do you guys ever see this when you read the New Testament? Jesus says a whole bunch of stuff and the disciples just walk away going: "Well, what does that mean?" And then he says things, it kinds of bums me out the way he says it to them, he goes, "Are you still so dull?" And I'm just like, "Yes, I am. Pleases give me some wisdom here." See, when you're doing personal ministry or your ministering under a word of knowledge you're walking with him, you're not trying to walk beyond him, where you don't move unless he gives more information.

So, if God's not giving you information, you don't have to overwhelm yourself with: "I'm not getting it." Because you can't get it. It's a spiritual truth. You won't discern it unless the Spirit reveals it to you. And you so you don't have to put this heavy bondage on yourself that you're not getting it. When I first started praying for people, just to give you an idea . . . . I used to stand around them, and again, people would say "Wow, do you see the Holy Spirit on that person." I'd just look at them and I thought, "Well, how do you see the Holy Spirit anyway?" I thought he was spirit, you know.

And then they just said, "No, you know, just let God fill your mind with these images," and stuff like that. But as I started praying with people I started realizing, even if I sit there and tell them this awesome picture that I have, there's no deliverance that comes to them. Have you ever done that? "Well, the Lord showed me that your dad beat you up when you were growing up." Well, they already knew all of that. That isn't going to deliver them of anything. Right? And so, I started realizing that this is just a process of how God starts getting information to you.

But at every level of this you decide how far you're going to go with him. You want me to test that out for you? Give you an example of that? I was complaining to the Lord one day about why he doesn't give me people's names. Because I was in a lot of Paul Cain meetings and I thought, "That's kind of cool." I'd like to get some names for people and tell them what they're favorite ice cream is and stuff like that, right? And so, what happens is when I go to meetings, people, either whether I'm tired or not, for some odd reason, they think, "Well, he's God's man of faith and power, so we're going to put him in a bedroom by himself." That's usually what happens to me all the time is that I'm forced into a quiet place whether I want to be or not. So, I'm stuck in this kid's room.

And I lay down and I thought, "Well, God, I guess I'd better pray to you a little bit about the meeting tonight." And instead of asking him questions and being nice to him, I started getting into a real bad attitude. I said, "You know, I don't like doing this anymore because you don't give me specific information. You seem to give it to everyone else and you make me struggle and there's a room of 200 people and I have to try to call them out by the color of their clothes. And since I'm color blind, I mess that up. And so, I have to try to figure some way of getting their attention." And I said, "Why don't you just give me someone's name and quit goofing around with me." Alright? I'm complaining. We call it prayer, alright? And I said, "Well . . ." I'd heard a tape by Paul Cain and Mike was interviewing him and asking him how he got them. And I thought, "Well, I guess you get a name like this." You get a name like Helen and Helen has two children and one child is growing in intercession and I'm just saying all of this. And I thought, and then you get something like "Bill." And Bill is a carpenter and he's having struggles financially. And the Lord's going to minister to him. And all of a sudden I could feel the presence of the Holy Spirit on me. And the Lord spoke to me and he said, "Well, that was me.

I'm telling you. Helen is out in the crowd. She has two children. She's going through financial problems." And I said, "Wait a minute. That's way too easy, God." Because the way you hear people talk about this: I had to be knocked down in a trance for God to give me this information. It couldn't just simply come to me. And I realized right there, I'd set up a stronghold in my mind that I couldn't receive it like other people could.

    I had to have this experience before God would speak to me that way. Does that making any sense? So I went to the meeting that night. I told this person, I said, "You know, I really don't want to do this. It's the first time I'm ever going to do this. I said, I feel like God gave me some people's specific name." And he goes, "Well . . ." And he put, he scared the tar out of me. He goes, "Well, you know that's a new level right there." And so, I'm already nervous out of my mind thinking, "I'm going to stand up here and make a total idiot out of myself." And when he said that, I just went, "Wow." But he said, "But, I'll call you up and you do it." And I thought, "I don't want to do this now.

    I want to go sit at the book table and sell tapes. I don't want to do this meeting tonight." So, we get up there and it's my time and he calls me up there and I just stand up there and I said, "Alright. Is there a lady named Helen?" Well, what's really funny is when I saw it actually in the picture that God gave me, she was sitting over here on this side of the sanctuary. And all of a sudden this lady stands up right here on this side of the sanctuary. Well I thought, "Well, that's way too easy."

You know, I thought I had to be gripped by the presence of the Holy Spirit. And have like this trance experience and then see her, right? She stood up and I said, "Your name's Helen." And she says, "Yes." And I thought, "What was I supposed to say again?" Because I didn't write it down. I usually try to write it down. And I thought, "Oh, now what am I supposed to say." And everyone's looking at me. And then I realized, and I said, "You have two children, don't you?" And she said, "Yes." And I said, "And this child's doing this . . ." And she said, "Yes." And I said, "And you've been struggling financially, haven't you?" And she said, "Yes." And all of a sudden the Father moved in and really started touching her and all I was giving her was words of knowledge and then he turned it into prophecy. And she came up to me after the meeting and she said, "You know, the most powerful thing was that God actually gave you my name."

Now, does that mean that now I'm in a league set apart from everyone else because I get names? No. I challenged the Lord to break down a stronghold in my mind, which was that I couldn't get names. And he just simply gave it to me. Now, guys, we do this all the time.

"I can't give words like that person." "I can't see like that person." "I can't do like that person." And, yes, you can. Are you ready?

If I'm telling you this right now and telling you that I'm able to come into this, God will stretch you to try to come into it also. Because, ministry is supposed to come among you and ministers are supposed to get you excited about this so you'll do.

Because God wants all of you walking into places and saying, "Oh, your name is Jane, isn't it? And your father's been having problems, hasn't he? And the Lord wants to minister to you." I mean, that's how the Lord wants to do it. And we say, "Well, that's only for that guy up there and he's set apart by God and I'll never be able to do that." That's nonsense.

Those gifts were given to the Body of Christ so you would move in them. Am I challenging you guys enough? Okay. So, yes, go ahead Now, one way that God does this is that he allows you to see pictures. That's how words of knowledge works. Another one is this: words or phrases given to you. This is a fun one. When God does this . . . now, this is where you have to learn the voice of the Lord. Especially when it comes to words of knowledge.

Sometimes he shows you pictures. Sometimes he just cuts all of that off and he wants to train you in a new way. And what he'll do is he'll just give you one word.

That's always . . . I love that one. And usually what it looks like is this. If I am in a room with people, or I'm praying for a group of people and I'll look at someone and I'll say, "Tell me something." And he'll give me a word. He'll say, "Tell that person I am hearing their prayers." And I say, "And . . ." Because anyone could say that. That doesn't really blow anyone out of the water when you say, "Well, God's hearing your prayers." "Is there anything else." what he does is he won't give you any more information. And if you press him, you find out there isn't any more information coming. Do you know why? Because what he's doing is he's getting you in a place of, "Now you've got to take the step over the wall of faith." Once you start taking that step, here comes a flow of revelation and all of a sudden you're caught in it. Now, that can happen with a word or phrase.

Or even before you even go to minister to a group of people . . . you could be laying in bed in the morning and he'll say, "Now there's a guy that you're going to meet. And you're going to say this, this and this to him." See, it can come both ways. We can't just get locked into a model of this. Now, does this challenge you guys at all? Or are you sitting around going I can't do this. I mean are you guys saying that? Don't do that, okay. I'm just trying to tell you examples of how you can start doing this stuff.Another one is this: Because words of knowledge, discerning of spirits and visionary revelation, they all work as a team on stuff, sometimes you feel stuff on your body and then he'll pop you right into having visions.

Or you'll hear a word with it. The first clear word of knowledge I ever had on healings and have you ever seen the Doans commercials they used to have in the early or mid-80's where they'd always show this guy . . . this cartoon of this guy's back and then they have an arrow and they go, "Pain." Alright, and then there would be a circle around that. And you knew that Doans was goanna actually heal this guy of this pain in his shoulder. Well, that was the first clear word of knowledge I got.

I just was looking at a person and I see this light around their shoulder and this Doans commercial arrow pointing at it and I thought, because I'm a visual type person, I thought, "Wo, that's really cool." Maybe I ought to go home and draw that or something like that. And I knew that that was an invitation to ask questions. You see, if it comes on you, the presence of God comes on you, you're open to hear it. And that also tells you something about your private time in prayer. You can't hear God unless he's on you or he's near you or he's present with you. It's just kind of hard to do that, okay? Now, what happens is God makes you feel things inside your spirit that produces words of knowledge. I was in Guatemala and that was really difficult because they don't speak English. And so, a lot of the jokes I can tell, no one got them. Most of the jokes I tell, no one gets anyway, but . . . especially down there. Every joke I told, the people would just look at me. And they always looked angry. I never could figure that out. And I and I caught Montezuma's Revenge. So, I did everything I could think of not to get Montezuma's Revenge and I got it the second day I was there. So, if I wasn't in the meeting, I was in the bathroom. Thank God, in the meeting the Holy Spirit would come on me and that would stop. But the minute the meeting would end, the first . . . me and this other kid would look and we'd see who could race the fastest to get to the bathroom. It was just a mess. Anyway, I have to tell you that to tell you this word of knowledge, okay? So, in the middle of the meeting I'm looking at this lady and I'm starting to feel this thing in my stomach, and I thought, I'm going to have Montezuma's Revenge right here. And so, I was trying to . . . I had the microphone in my hand.

I'm telling you all this to explain my reactions to my next word of knowledge. In the meeting as I looked at this lady, I began feeling the upset stomach. I thought I would have an accident right there. I began to realize that if I stopped looking at the lady the pain stopped. I thought maybe she had it too but that didn't fit so I asked the Lord if she was sick like me and He said no. What you're feeling is actually the pain she feels concerning her daughter.

Immediatley pictures began coming like a movie screen in my mind.

I see this little child . . . now, this is hard, you're looking at a person and you're actually having a movie screen going on in your mind. I'm looking at this little kid and I'm watching the kid praying and I'm looking at the mother and I'm realizing she's having pain over this child. And then I see a picture on the other side of her praying for this child. And then I see this child running all over the house, screaming and yelling and she can't get control of the child. And I said, Okay, I see all of that. What do you want me to do with it?" And he wouldn't tell me anything. And I realized, okay, now that means I have to step out and start talking about this with this lady. So I said, "Ma'am, you have a daughter, don't you?" And she said, "Yes." And right when I said that there was a word of knowledge that popped in my spirit and I said, It's actually your youngest child, because you have several." And she said, "That's right." I said, "That child . . ." and all of a sudden the first thing that was brought up in my mind through a word of knowledge was the child running around the house.

And so, I realize that's what I have to go with. I say, "This child drives you up the wall." Now, she didn't understand what that meant. In Guatemala we don't have the same phrases, and she looked at me like: "Drive you up the wall?, what does that mean? And I don't own a car.

What is that phrase?" And so, I had to rephrase it. I said, "The child gets on your nerves. The child drives you . . . not drives you up the wall . . . but, makes you want to pull your hair out."

She understood that phrase. And she said, "Yes." And I said, "But, you know what? The spirit of intercession that's actually resting on you. . .,"because that second image came up, and I knew that was what I was supposed to go with, and I said, "Actually, you've been praying for the child." And she said, "Yes." And I said, "Actually, the spirit of intercession that's resting on you . . ." And she said, "Yes.". . . is actually coming on that child." Now she started crying right there. And I said, And all this stuff that you've been fighting and struggling with thinking that that child's rebellious . . .

Now, I'm hearing the Lord say this, "Tell her, that child's not rebellious. That child is a burden-bearer and just like her, and the reason it bugs her so much is because she sees herself in the child." And after I started telling her that, you could tell the Lord just descended on her and gave her knowledge for why she could hardly stand her youngest daughter. But all that came as a series of feeling something and then knowledge came out of it.

Now, let's go here. We said this last week. This information that God gives is to bring faith in the people that God is moving. That's why word of knowledge is so powerful and why you want to sharpen it. Because it gives the people an ability . . . wait a minute, there's no way that guy knows that. And what it does is it causes their heart . . . Word of knowledge is almost like prophecy and the realization that it causes faith to energize them. The Holy Spirit starts landing on them. And also it does another thing. It starts developing hope in their inner man.

That God is actually going to come in their midst, in their immediate life, and answer questions that they've been confused about. See, that's why word of knowledge is actually a very great tool to use even in conflict resolution. Because God comes in the midst and explains something with which you have great difficulty and gives you simple information. Now, let's talk about the steps to walk in the gift. Again, most of them, and I'm going to say this on every one of them, you have to ask for the gift. Yes. Well, actually, I had a wrong concept with nonbelievers for a long time. I felt they were the guinea pigs to learn spiritual gifts. And so, that was a wrong concept I had. But I figured, these guys don't know what's going on anyway, so I'm just going to start asking them questions and saying things to them, just to get a shock response out of them. I had a real bad attitude for a long time towards nonbelievers because I didn't understand that Satan was my enemy, not the nonbelievers. And so, I thought the nonbelievers gave me grief, so I was going to give them grief back with spiritual gifts. And so, I don't know if that's going to thrill anybody, but that was my maturity level at that point in my life. And so, what you're supposed to do with nonbelievers is you're supposed to, again, just like we're doing with the church, you're to welcome them into this stuff. But, remember something. They have no grid for any of this. Okay? And so, you're going to say something like, I feel like the Lord showed me something." Most of them don't even believe there is a God and so they're going to struggle with that. And so, it's always good to first . . . I'm telling you a reverse strategy, it's always good first to really get sharp in the gift as you're moving out into the world. Do it in home groups all the time or do it as much as you can, so that when you go out in the world you are getting correct information. Lord telling me this about you. Or showing me this stuff." And just share it with them. See, the reason why gifts aren't accepted both in the church and out of the church is because of the way we demonstrate them. If you just share information with people, they can either say yes or no. Another interesting thing, I decided, like Gary is talking about, let's go into the work place with this. This is so much fun in the home groups, let's see what happens with nonbelievers. Okay? So, I went to work one day and I was just sitting there drawing my stuff that I had to do for the week and all of a sudden my throat started hurting really bad.

And thought, "Wo, what is that?" I mean, it just came on me. And I went, Okay, now, I'm not sick. What is this?" And I said, "God, what is that?" And he said . . . now, I didn't hear this audible voice. I just realized this is an anointing because I could feel the Holy Spirit on me and then this pain was associated with it. So, I just started looking around the room and I thought, I wonder who that's for?" All of a sudden, I look over in the next cubicle and this lady's right there . . . and he goes, "That's the lady. Go pray for her." And I said, "Well, okay, I will. But what's causing that thing?" And then he shows me this demon sitting on this lady's back. And I didn't want . . . why did I ask that? And so, I said, "Well, I see that." And so I walked over there and I said, "You know. . .," I interrupted her work and made her take her headphones off and I said, "Hey, do you have a sore throat? And it's hurting right here and it goes down your throat on this side?" And she says, "Yeah, I do." And I said, "Well, the Lord showed me that and I'd like to pray for you." And she said, Okay." And so, I started praying for her, "Holy Spirit, just bring your power and start healing her." And when I did this, I

have this vision of this demon turning his head and looking at me. So, I'm looking at it and the Lord says, "He's not going to go until you rebuke it." And I thought, "How can you rebuke a demon, something that doesn't even believe in the Lord?" And so, I said, "Come here." She got up and I said, I'm going to say a bunch of stuff. Don't listen to me, okay?" I said, "Just close your eyes and I'm just going to pray for you." And so I put my head/hand ? behind her back, like this, and I said, [in a purposely muffled voice] "In the name of Jesus Christ, come out." And she goes, "What?" And I said, "Nothing, I was just clearing my throat." And when I did that the demon left her. Alright? And she started getting healed. And she said,

"No, seriously, what was that you said?" Now, I had no wisdom, and I thought, well she'll understand this, because she just got healed. I said, "Actually, it was a demon that was making you sick." And she goes, "A demon!" Okay, now, guys, the Lord just healed her, all right? She started making fun of me because I said that. Almost to the point where she's literally healed, but she couldn't accept that fact, so that I had to go end up sitting back in my cubicle and for the rest of the day she went around the office and told everybody, "Brian said I had a demon on me." And [imitating everyone laughing at him]. These religious people.

Well, God healed her right there on the spot. God actually healed her and she spent the rest of the day persecuting me because of that. Yes, go ahead. [Brian takes question from audience. Question cannot be heard on tape]. Well, that's a good question. I don't know. In my attempts of trying to do that, I've run into a lot of different scenarios. I've found that specifically in that one I had to address it or nothing was going to happen. A lot of times I don't ever tell anybody . . . first, the minute you start saying that you move in revelation and you say, I just saw a demon over you," everyone just looks at you like, I can't believe they haven't caught this guy yet." You know.

And so, most of the time unless I have to specifically address it, and I had to with this lady, you can just command the demon to leave without even mentioning its name, just by addressing the affliction and so, I guess it just depends. See, it depends on the situation and how you feel God's leading you to do it. There isn't any specific method. Again, I told you that story for the realization not only that that was fun, but also because of my immaturity on how to deal with nonbelievers. And a lot of them aren't ready for you to say, "Well, ya, an angel just came and stood right beside you." I mean, they're just not ready for that.

What they need is just God to do what he's going to do and then let them deal with the realization of that. The reason that God allowed me to do that is later on I found out that this lady actually had dreams all the time. I mean supernatural dreams that were from an evil spirit realm that God wanted me to address later in her life as I kept working with her. And even though she hated me that day for saying that, it started bugging her and made her start going on this search for God. So, that's why I believe he made me address it the way he did. Okay, now, be willing take risks with receiving gifts to help people. There isn't a place when you do this that you will not have to do that. Again, in all my time trying to do this kind of stuff, I've come to the conclusion that it's always about risk. That's the word faith. Faith in action and risk.

But you can take some of the sting away from the risk if you learn to be gentle and have a sense of humor. If you have to be right and dogmatic, you're going to get creamed a lot. I used to try to be right and dogmatic and when people didn't want to, see . . . let me say something . . . even in the church, a lot of people aren't ready for a God that's in their face, right now. Let's say that I'm dealing with an issue and I'm wounded about it. And you get a word of knowledge and you come up to me and you go, "Here's what the Lord's showing me about you." It might actually be truth, but you don't like . . . I don't know about you guys . . . but do a lot of you guys go to the grocery store and just rip off your clothes and stand in front of everybody and go, "Look at this scar." Well, some of you must, I mean, no one responded to that one, anyway. But see, that's what it's like when the Holy Spirit comes and confronts you about something. You just feel like, "My God, I'm exposed to everybody." And some people aren't ready to deal with it here and now. And so, if you're actually accurate, they'll blow you off.

And you have to learn to have a sense of humor about some of this stuff. And that will actually help people come into the things of God. But if you're just . . . you know, I'm going to use a weird phrase, if you're just Pentecostal when you do it: "You accept this!" Well, it's going to be harder for them to deal with. And it's hard for God to be right in your face saying, "You know, I know you're grocery shopping right now, but you're going to deal with this." And so, you have to have a sense of humor.

What I do is, I try to tell a series of silly jokes, just to relax everybody, so that God can come and minister to them. And talk about how, you know, I don't know if this is right, or if it isn't." Just trying to relax it enough, because if it is a word of knowledge and it's true, God will make the impact right there in front of you. I mean, you just don't really have to add to it.

I believe that if you're called to be a disciple of the Lord Jesus Christ, this is my assumption from reading the New Testament, you will go through seasons where he'll train you to hear for a while and then he'll stop it. And then he'll awaken visionary revelation. Then he'll stop that and then he'll go back to trying to get both of them to work at the same time. See, growing in maturity is hearing God at every level that he's made available for you. Not just trying to stay in one vein, okay? So, if you do have ability to hear him right now, there will come a season in your maturity where he'll let that wane and he'll awaken you to visionary revelation and train you in that for awhile. Because, if you look at how the disciples did ministry later in the Book of Acts, especially Peter and those guys, you could tell that they had spent time with Jesus.

And what I mean by that is, they not only saw things, they heard things. They were actually able to move in all the ways that revelation came in and that told you that they were trained correctly by the Lord. Now, he does the same thing today. He takes you in an area that you're comfortable with and he says, "You know, they're way too comfortable in this. I need to train them." So, he stops that arena to awaken you into another arena, where you can see. Now, you don't have to try to do it, he'll just bring it on you when it's time. Does that make sense?

What I try to do is this. Whenever I feel the presence of the Lord, if God is not giving you information again, you don't have to worry about it. It just means that, Oh, God's here. Even though this is just normal talk, God is energizing something here in this conversation that I'm having with this person. And so you don't have to worry if he's . . . don't . . . see, I always ask, "Show me something.""Say something to me." And if he doesn't give it, I just don't worry about it. I'm just trying to become a disciple that's willing to serve and if he doesn't want to give me information, that's what he's called me to do is just to sit and listen and not worry about the results, because that's up to him.

And so, a lot of times, I feel the presence of the Lord . . . I mean, do you ever do this . . . drive down the road and all of a sudden there's the presence of the Lord. You're thinking, "What am I supposed to do with this?" Most of the time you're not supposed to do anything about it except just receive it. Oh, this is God loving me. He's coming here and he's embracing me, he's hugging me and kissing me and telling me I'm his own. I mean, that's a lot of what that stuff is. For a long time I thought, every time I feel any anointing of the Holy Spirit I've got to look for somebody, because that's the person ?. But, if you're ever doing 75 miles an hour on the highway and trying to stop to give a word of knowledge to somebody ñ it's really difficult. And so, you have to have an ease with God about this stuff.

Sometimes it is for someone and sometimes it's just for you. And God just wants to give you information or just encourage you that you're a faithful child and so that's why he does that. To activate you into words of knowledge because you have to have knowledge of what it is. But it's coupled with discerning of spirits, because you're able to have that revelation going on.

Does that make sense? It's like, discerning of spirits and words of knowledge and words of wisdom kind of walk in hand-in-hand. It's kind of hard to just cut this apart and say, "That's that, and that's that." They kind of energize each other into revelation. And so, if I have a vision, I'm discerning something. Because I'm having a vision and God's opening my eyes into the spirit realm. Then he gives information that leads towards words of knowledge and then he's looking for the effect of it.

See, when you're having revelation . . . I don't know if you guys have ever done this? You start getting revelation and you look around and you're going, "This is not what's going on in the room right now." This is a hard concept, but I'm going to try to explain it. When the Spirit of God comes, he's eternal.

Because he's eternal, he'll tell you about stuff now, that has nothing to do with anything, but it might be something that you need to pay attention to that's going to help you two weeks from now. And it's learning to not go with anything and just receiving it until God tells you it's time to do something with it. Like, many times when the spirit of revelation is resting on me, he's not talking to me about what's going on in this room, or not in this room, I mean, in a group of people I'm ministering with. And I'll say, "Well, tell me something about that." And he'll say, I don't want to talk to you about that. I want to talk to you about what's going to be coming up in the next two years." And I'm like, "Why now?" It's because he chooses what he's going to talk to me about and how I'm to receive it and what I'm to do with it.

When I get into word of knowledge next time we come back, I'll bring them all three together and show you how it can go into . . . now, see . . . Kenneth Hagin believes words of wisdom is for the future. Other people believe word of wisdom is to take word of knowledge and learn how to apply it now. So, there's a lot of different ways that you can view words of wisdom and they all do work in those arenas. So, we'll talk about it when we get back from vacation, but yes and no. It just depends on what's going on at the time. It's God training you to do stuff. The only way that I can say that I've gotten relaxed with it is, I'm going and praying for people a lot. Sometimes, I just say, "God, let's just cut to the quick here, what am I supposed to be doing with this person?" And then a series of thoughts will come to me and I'll say, "Well, that's kind of interesting." And then I'll just write them down. I don't see the person for two weeks. I go there and it's time to minister and all of a sudden all that stuff he told me floats

What Are Words of Knowledge

right back up into my system. See, we have given our lives to the Lord, so he uses us and, remember, he's building in us all the time.

Now, I don't think, well, I don't know if I want to use the word "crud," but I think some of it could be random, but remember that God is always building line upon line in your life. And so, it might not make sense here at this level, but when he's built up to this level, it makes sense. And so, you have to be willing to let God sift you. See, when I'm getting words of knowledge always at the end of the day, again, I'm reviewing them, "Is that really for something or is that just me because I was thinking about Disneyland and then this thought came in. And I let him prune me. And I say, If it isn't for me, just take it away. Just bring death to that on the cross and let the power of the cross bring to light what you're really trying to tell me.

Brian Fenimore and his wife, Kellie, are founders of Plumbline Ministries, an organization based in Kansas City, Missouri, dedicated to releasing power in the Kingdom of God through preaching the gospel, healing the sick, deliverance and miracles. Pastoring for 20 years, Brian was brought forth in 1997 into an itinerant role of equipping leaders and churches. He has traveled extensively across North America, teaching and imparting the power of prayer, prophetic ministry and destiny and healing. The author additional study materials and many teaching in video and audio form. He was a teacher in the School of the Spirit of Grace Training Center, Kansas City, Missouri, and founder of Plumbline Training Institute. He and Kellie have been married for 32 years and three children.
For more information:

Brian Fenimore
www.plumblinem.com

CPSIA information can be obtained
at www.ICGtesting.com
Printed in the USA
LVHW101430211221
706736LV00024B/381